Cicadas

Serenade

CICADAS SERENADE

A Romeo Nation
Copyright 2021

CONTENTS

CICADAS SERENADE

The Most Peculiar Way

I stall for crystal creations that came during the night
I listen to the speckled globes that glisten through frost bite
brittle branch stands little chance against weight of beauties dance
a last lament so heaven sent, an ornament perchance

this happenstance romance of winters whimsical allure
gives me much hope for all the things that prior seemed unsure

the storm will torment dormant fears and chill us to the bone
but what a sight the pearly white that one day might be shown
if only we can last the night, we might see light of day
through suffering comes beauty in the most peculiar way

Bella Gone

Behold! Behold! the plants unfold to be with you and I
as we sit beneath the oak with my hand upon your thigh
leaves of lightest green are seen between what once was white
insects now crawl and fly about and seek to take a bite

I ask if you will listen but you do not wish to hear
[my measured words in meter truly met her greatest fear]

I should have weighed the pros and cons of confession in prose
but now an unrequited love is all that this heart knows
I no longer enjoy the birds, nor care for songs they sing
loves roundabout misfortune circles belles without a ring

Drain Storm

I watch the waves that cars can form while driving in the street
I try to make the largest splash by stomping with my feet
as leaves become these pirate ships that race to edge of earth
they get trapped in the whirlpool and I ponder treasures worth

beyond the grate of filtered fate, I know I am not sane
I have never been the same since my life went down the drain

I've clogged my tears from coming out I never really grieve
this overflowing emotion for all of those who leave
the traffic in my mind keeps blaring horns of my have nots
my poems serve as puddles for collecting all my thoughts

Onward Poets

Onward weary poet, do not falter
the feather plume shall bloom this world once more
alter life to lie upon thine altar
and wave to sand that stands beside the sure

Onward wary poet, head without heed
the wind shall never whine for lack of flight
if ego floods thy chasm, supersede!
for angels do not always glisten white

In words we wear our sentiment on sleeve
through pallet we bring color to this age
let pendulum of pensive natures weave
and dance us through this ever-passing stage

In words we war but never stand to win
for all the poets battle from within

Unraveled Raven

Come hither with her my withered worry
be not sorry for thy surly sermon
serpents surely seek to usurp vermin
by virtue of squirming worm in jury

Bury away this fear of death that lurks
out of sight, out of mind, yet right behind!
what's left of knowledge when we reach the rind?
through logic god is killed so science works

unearth the worth of words that poets write
for life extends much further than the grave
confined beneath an epitaph we slave
to unravel why ravens rave at night

and here I sit and ponder without care
I see you not, but know that you are there

Such an Hour is This

Mayhaps my lapse of judgement hence
is why I stand on unpicked fence
   yet pick it or not
   this is my spot
the unwashable hand that feeds my thought
how fanciful these fears that interrupt so abrupt
if I were not a more prudent student
I might erupt
   But in the dormant throws of volcanos
   the village rarely knows
   if lava flows beneath the crust
from ashen passion to heated lust
there is no one I can trust
for even my mind is not immune to rust
   Yet I humor it now
   as I speak with it
perhaps some lucky passersby
will assume I've lost my wit
and commit me to some commune of Christ
   but sanity rarely speaks at such an hour
   for the shadows of night do much to empower
   and I care not for the show nor the shower
I don't wish to be clean
   I wish to devour virgin flower that grows in me
   for although I know it is read
I bleed
   I am but a weed
   in this whimsical garden of need
   and I grow weary
   in this quagmire query of who I am
why do I ask when I already know
why can I not say
why can't I let go

Genderless Voice

Rejoice!
For I am the genderless voice of a generation of choice…cuts of meat

I am the discrete treat you secrete your secret regret into
for I am two
I am the duality fatality of fragile masculinity
I am the divinity of the divide
and I will provide

for 200 HH
and 500 VIP

Pogo Stick

Poe, go stick your heart beneath the floor
can't you see the ravens sore?
this sour hour; forevermore
craven flight; we never soar
or will our oar sure the shore
only Tom will tell

as time shall wane, we shame Mark Twain
for trains of thought and racial rot

if facial recognition
can capture horrid spot
then who shall wash this Macintosh
when sinful natures caught

Digital Affirmations

I fidget in my seat, as my digital affirmations fail to meet the lowest of my expectations. How can something as small as a decimal decimate me so. I am numb from the number that haunts this slumber. I am the clammy hand calamity of virtue vanity…how pathetic this path of pity I pursue…am I still me…or do I sound like you?

The Great I AM

Am I shepherd
or am I lamb?
if god was man
am I I AM?

why oh why is this doubt so loud
how is it crowd can shrug off shroud
and precipitate in a fate outside of cloud

Speck

I am not special
I am a speck
within the spectrum
of humdrum hymns
of hope

Snowflake Poets

Ensnared I sneer at the fear I should feel
impaired despair is a rare thing to spare
and yet we spar in this rhapsodic zeal
of zephyrs and heifers that truncate air

Hell, if phantoms could foster imposter
perhaps the sheets of white have power yet
me thinks my inks do slink with the Froster
two roads of urge diverge and hold regret

Mayhaps peddled flowers of May may die
if a mayday of melody decry
but if we forage through what is our rage
the folly of the fall can come of age

for even seasoned poets didn't know
how fake the flake could feel within the snow

Atom and Eve

I can't rescind the wind of betrayals
so long as valiant valence prevails
to hold my energy captive in you
for you have stolen part of me, it's true

this veil hence has masked what is the matter
tabled thought of tea for this mad hatter
this period of odd tickles my sense
how noble can I be to jump the fence?

for [He] who changes voice to reach high pitch
shall [O] the trees for air he didn't take
in [Au] of other love we see as rich
whose elemental bonds we cannot break

new tones are found in apples that deceive
how fitting that all atoms have an eve

Frosted Roads

I concede I sowed the seed
for I saw a need to erode the road
but foolish me could not foresee
I paved the way for poet's ode

and frosted road enhanced the cracks
for which my isolation lacks
a day when sickle seemed so fickle
lackadaisical the tracks

Sanctuary of Sinners

I am sanctuary of sinners, thus…
passion can pour through my poisonous sting
I'm the ill lust in the trio of us
the illustrious will to kill the king

where pearly gates meet twisted fates of fools
and spools of dead do wind my dreadful thread
we carve pidge in where doves do sit on stools
and shadow dusks upon thy marble head

I am hell bent intent that is serpent
the overflowing cup of pent-up pride
yet YOU so heaven sent have brought content
for which my callous nature can confide

what harm can demonic harmonic sing
when angels flutter down on golden wing

Porcelain Pinocchio's

Porcelain Pinocchio's
crack under their lies
in lieu of all they rue I knew
they couldn't compromise

the polished glaze on china doll
makes for shiny eyes
yet fragile are the games they play
that lead to their demise

Ecce Homophone

I'm king of con
hard R in ape
the superego without a cape
ecce homophone take shape
how queer is death that carry sape

two tutus are far too much
for dancing queens that carry crutch
kickstand stands erect for kick
as bi cycles perform a trick

turned out for poetic pimp
this masochistic diction's limp
a treasure trove of damning drivel
that salivates to sit and swivel

Funeral Fun

So eerie are these thoughts that won't conform
and yet I wish to be queer ear of worm
I wish to hear the voice of deathly form
I do not squirm at stiffs who lie their firm

for lie they do in boxes of deceit
how long can breath be held from six feet deep?
what hunger is in heart that seeks to eat
the sorrows of the widow that can't sleep?

phony money moans at ceremony
the will will instill will for friends to come
the matradee serves Krafty macaroni
and in the back, amazing grace is strum

a ruse like this could only come from thee
but you can stop pretending dad…it's me

Foreverwhore

Societies rapidly veering to vapid
and fleshing out its carnal core
I see the eyes that don't see me
and fade me out forever more

So ravenous the tapping thought
tap me
tap me
and love me not

Within a Coo

To rest my head against your arm
to char myself within your charm
to harm my heart and let it sing
to singe myself within this fling

And then to think nothing of it
for eyes are closed and lip is bit
and flush is face like crimson rose
for floor is dressed in all our clothes

And none of this needs overstating
purity is palpitating
for all that I should know of you
is understood within a coo

Yet foolish me will try to write
and capture beauty of this night

Wax Poetic

To warm my heart, I speak thy name
as shadows dance and feel no shame
flicker quicker my fickle flame
wax poetic and know thy game

melt they love across my skin
burn my wants in white hot sin
through dimming light and rising din
I feel thy flame that burns within

hurry now, our time draws nigh
suffocate this sirens sigh
snuff my muff until I cry
let thy love run down my thigh

string your pearls from wicked wick
I pity candles that burn too quick

Our Brothers Keeper

We live in a generation petrified into believing the genocide of our liberties is the only path to a prosperous tomorrow. Yet it is not the harsh rhetoric of a slamming fist that insists we genuflect. Instead, it is the open palm of the ever-calm beggar that robs us blind. Cloaked in the falsehoods of altruism, the ayes pocket our sympathetic aesthetic. Our eye sockets plugged into mischievous media thugs that usher in a new age of sage clarity. We are asked to ignore the sin in sincerity as death marches in. The rasputinesc reaper reminds us how we are our brothers' keeper…the fate of the state grows deeper and deeper.

Water Down the Pain

It pains me when they water down the paint
don't they see the beaty they've destroyed
for ease of sell the easel was employed
to showcase sinners masking as if saint

and yet the most horrendous part in this
is knowing that I might have done the same
I had my dose of whore and with it came
the same, in knowing love bereft of kiss

this Pollock pride precipitates in words
for callous was the nature they were thrown
so many kings yet none of whom are known
posts spar with "Spear" and fall on swords

and yet we are no sharper for this duel
for poets young and old will break a rule
and add a line too many...like a fool

Period Peace

How exquisite the visit
although, we know just visage
only stone can atone what is a mirage.

A myriad of meaning
a period appears
if sentence should end, then shouldn't my fears?

Squid Squo Pro

Cellophane pod
that shoots to the moon
and gravitates towards impending doom

cephalopod
that swims in the deep
secrete ink secret
that you alone keep

On Facing Writer Block

Drink
get hammered…
and grab a chisel

every block
is an opportunity
to carve out the truth in your art
leave the brittle chunks of unworthy material
scatter all over the floor

sculpt
your masterpiece

Madness in Flesh

How now
the howling horror of this baseless home
pray stilts may yet find will to hold
the hollow fellow I follow
will willow wallow or will it weep

within these waking dreams I pray to keep
the shrieking sound of sleepless night at bay
oh, why must I obey the will of sway
and say what I don't mean

could I not reconvene with the scene of sorrow
the shattered day that is tomorrow
or has shepherded lost his flock
like time to melting clock

if past is out to pasture
then where is the crook
where will we look
when shear madness dances in our flesh

Sex on It

This brainwashed stain that seeps into our sleep
behind the smoke and mirrors, we still lack
we wax and wane the sane we feign to keep
and coddle creature comforts till we crack

how soon will moon consume the crescent care
this howling urge emerges like the wind
the scent of sentimental thoughts compare
to those who re-sinned after they rescind

scintillating gleams of broken light dance
upon the seams from ripples in a trance
disturbing surface level has a price
we chew and screw all virtue into vice

verbally we vex our complex hex
when all that we could really want is sex

Just a Draft

Daft freewill, we laughed adrift
in effervescent playful lift
the scent of sinful grin-full gift
that stole my heart in petty grift
engraving letters all to swift
and grafting souls with goals to sift
the golden years

our seasoned love still holds the thrill
of secret notes we left in draft
and every single daffodil
reminds me of the way we laughed

Prey Tell

Kneeling belle knell beneath the swell
of swollen gland and **muf**fled yell

I pray
no man will tell
I am the prey
beside mantel
[how odd to define where fire should dwell]

why of why do I settle for this
why am I more like Matisse
and less like mantis
I am mantic…and yet I roam
I have no place
you call me **home**

poor ceiling
poor ceiling
poor ceiling
glass

porcelain
porcelain
porcelain
ass

Behind the Shade

Do I cavort with the distorted cavity of my depravity
just to get my fill in?
or do I sit and spin around this sin with glee
how Krafty
the single me invented thee
to intermingle happily
and to destroy worlds
without stepping outside

but I'll let you decide
if the blinds stay shut for another cut
or if my memory should fade
behind the shade

Spineless Sin

I splinter from my spinless sin
I don't know how to let you in
to me

I come undone yet I'm compelled
you're everything that can't be held
you're free

K-Dense

u/ u/ u/ u/ u/
do I defy silence of sheep and lamb
u/ u/ u/ u/ u/
to stress the great I am within iamb
/u /u /u /u /u
trochee broke thee counter like a tyger
/u /u /u /u /u
radiate the form with eye on Geiger

/ uu/ uu/ u/
I doth protest if anapest should fit
/ uu/ uu/ u/
yet understand we interrupt for wit

/uu u /uu /uu
man's akin to mannequins' manic kin
u /uu u /uu //
how prominent is dactylic therein
u /uu u /uu uu
we're too afraid to overthrow the flow
u /uu /uu /uu
when buffalo buffalo buffalo

perhaps if I were to write on spondee
the lack of spontaneity would show
let's turn the hassle over and agree
that cadence isn't all that one should know

Long Gone

Long gone are the rainy days
we stood by the window and listened

we had nothing to account for
aside from connecting the dots
between all the innocent drops
that were momentarily suspended
from their ultimate destination

Never Sway

what do we leave behind
what story do we tell
through unkempt words that fall pell-mell

hell is bound by more than flame
…and yet every poet seeks a name

through iceberg theory
or weary spiel
readers know just how to feel

yet writers focused on how to spell
hold all the bells that never knell

oh well

belles get credit but know not the toll
weighted dice rebuke their role

fading roots shall not rue the soot
of a burning importance that truncated their stay
even if I had more to say…you would never sway
and that is why you will be left breathless
in my absence

Bucket

My sale is full
of self-betrayal
how hollow the hull
this lull in me
a past amassed
the vacant see
this vexing sex
behind the veil
how fraught and over thought this wail
how frail...and pail

kicked

Bending Beauty

though we may get high
on our supple supply
not everyone will understand
the dangers of the bends
in beauty

The Image of Suffering

My words never mattered...
not when compared to the battered beauty
of shadows
dancing beneath feet
and claiming only a seat
        that rightfully should have always been theirs
heirs without ears don't fear the air of winter
splintering the woulds and coulds of ICE
against the niceties of vice
and the underlying price
that everything has

but what are words worth
if the author doesn't fit
        the images of suffering they conjure

Tap Out

How odd the ode
of remorse code
the tap tap tapping
in its morose mode
erodes the roads I chose
to drive myself mad

Flowers Sway; Lovers Chase

I will remember the place, though I might forget the way
on that windy autumn day when sun warmed my face
heart started to race as minds ran astray
lost in our grace…never to stay
flowers sway; lovers chase
misplace all gray
lay…trace

remember the place

In Lieu of Lie

All is well in lieu of lie
all that's true shall rue my why
let savant-garde discard this flame
this chagrin rind my charred remain
let mane of sane now mar the mare
this hairline crack that is despair
for pairs are flush with flippant pride
yet cards are dealt
they don't decide

Rind and Reason

I have no appeal
I am nothing but rind
the heinous mind of a fiend confined
   [do not slip]
  Do NoT SLip
DO Not LeT Her sLip Away
   (what did I say?)
why are these bars so cold today?

I grin and bear, then howl and bay
the heathen heart still can't obey
how foul this stay in my disarray
my disarray
disarray

…sorry

RATional Pride

elaborate my dear lab rat
orate on you labors and make fiction of fate
tell us of the cheese you ate
and how you watched your brothers die
while you feasted

the only thing that trickles down
is the shit from a fed rat

put up partitions and protect yourself
until you are the last rat in the maze
and then speak of grace

Decompose

I lie
for I lack
yet spring too me back
to a time when life was more vibrant than act

I am a suit without place
a weed in glass case
and my frail vail does not prevail
on this trail that is my trial

suitcase packed
I drink the vial
and compile this final thought
before the would or should can rot
and then I erase it all

Hatless and Helpless

I plead and plod with my need for a god
yet shoulder boulder to outlast atlas
I follow white habits as mountains thawed
I drank the tea to remain me; hatless

from crustacean to crucifix, we pray
and flood our minds with thoughts that we create
we do not push, yet empty swings still sway
like childhood dreams we gave up for a fate

prophets bank on unsure men who whimper
and limp along through life with help of crutch
Satan cannot help but simply simper
at new age thoughts that fall so out of touch

a ring of truth the hovers over head
is painted on the souls of all the dead

Mockingbird

Still petrified of things that lurch in night
as terror drips like sweat upon the sill
pray tell, am I the prey to tell of fright?
what creatures perch upon the birch to kill?

the white of terrors bark is on my face
yet images of horror do not flinch
the demon inches closer in his chase
it's no use as this nuanced noose doth cinch

my shortened breath forms clouds just like a train
as tunnel vision narrows arrows path
I harken back the dark before the rain
but cannot ring out belle through all my wrath

the doctor places Rorschach down to talk
why do they always set the cuckoo clock to mock?

A Poets Job

It is a poet's job
to document the scent of a cent
to retain the sentiment of an event
and thereby monetize ones Monet eyes
but the moan of a stone thrown is but a guise
for guys and girls despise the lies of lines
and how a poet defines
what is felt,
silk or cotton
but don't get caught
on how a poet strings you along
life is but a song

Moth Bawls

I want to close off this fantasy
for with the clothes off
the fantasy is gone
yet in my drawer there is a draw
between how I feel
and who you saw
I have no control of the hole in my soul
where the moth doth gnaw
but to let her fly
would be to deny
unsightly I
candy
coat
suicide note

Cod is Dead

If cod can but change his tune
and get the nod to boo the boon
a rotten life that carries mold
through bottled feelings that go unsold
will be re-souled

if god can but change his itch
to forsake poor and scratch the rich
we may just notice footprints hide
when carnal cravings break our stride
still…everything untrue is tried

this ode in code doth coddle the reader
so hollow the leader that follows the model
by breaking wind like Aristotle
we mask the gas
then hit the throttle

Trochilidae

Trochilidae that flew by night
spectre wings in search of nectar
while humming songs of pure delight
and spreading life while feasting too
your beauty caught in fleeting sight
drawn together within a charm
woke within me and urge to write
penning lines of virtues vector
that you had taught within your flight

Of Butterfly and Moth

While thinking of things
like the powdered wings
of butterfly and moth

there came this new thought
in beauty that's sought
but not
      cut from the same cloth

The Book of Jobs

for womb
this hell tolls
as the freewill fire drill consumes our souls
did we beg to begotten in the fog of forgotten?
was the apple always so bitter and rotten
beset with regret despite praise we receive
adamant Steve still took his leave
but not before damning us all

Sirens Sigh

I have sat in satin sheets where Satan's view is trident true
and I watched sodden angels cling to horseman carcass like glue
spineless men see not the harm, and lie with wingless words that fly
who am I to deny the callous calling of sirens sigh?

World through Wit

Cartesian craft came
long before cart
a liaison of lessons and lesion in heart
art is not well unless the eyes swell
compassion compels this artesian well
and what fell…but a saline orb
methinks there's a metaphor here to absorb
let's see what could fit
will you bite this orbit?
the world as we know
is whirled through our wit
we whittle out meaning
as chromosomes split

Isn't it Byronic?

In this fallacious homeostasis
between transcendental and flirtatious
we find and interstellar resting place
were glacial angels fuck and fall from grace

we ask the lord "what shouldn't we romance?"
will wood not rot through seedy thought of plants
we pull down pants and skirt with our free love
these bees all buzz with stinging thoughts of dove

we speak with Beelzebub in pub most foul
for cocks can make one's head spin like and owl
but lets us not think deeply, rue, or stir
when pleasure is a past of who we were

mother nature and I meld into one
how Oedipal it is that I'm her son

For rest

Some dream of branching out
I dream of childhood
yet slumber is in rooted fear
for rest lies in the would

Nevers Art

do I defy the stye in me?
as cradles rock
then turn to sand
and fall into the sea

if phantom fears should feed the hand
and stymie time
would you then stand
apart
from the art you never start

or would you command the colors
to run

Mea Culpa

Scrupulous artist chiseled and hammered
culpable sculpture; beauty enamored
sponges absorb absurd sore we spew
spontaneous us that share how we view

encased in glass we protect art from dust
the thing we become, despite fleshy trust
the crowds assemble and quickly disperse
the quivering lips of pain match the purse

as time marches on the cracks start to form
the river runs dry long after the storm
lifesaving water will vanish through doubt
without crying tears, we live life in drought

and yet connections outlive the giver
when rusted bridges fall without river

The Majesty

Why do prophets let me wade
            in all that I bemoan
how do I dissuade my shade
            from casting stone alone
I can't untie for noose has frayed
            while standing on my throne
I kick the chair of my despair
the Majesty unknown

What Leaves

beset with ill regret
this fragment scent of fall
the colors have all faded
will the wind no longer call?

as desolation fills my lungs
its escapes in foggy breath
how cold the heart can be
strip me naked to my death

But Never Heels

-Lashing out
-eye fashion
-a smile

she wears despair
but never heels
and yet she still lets
oh so many look up her hurt

stares
bring her another step closer
to being just another case
        so cheeky
        we blush
        and debase

Where We Stop

I stopped where path and river met
and thought of stones that never set
and then I thought of what was said
by settled rock on river bed
and there I saw the willow weep
for leaves that had no will to steer
my surface thoughts became more clear
as I myself did take a leap

My Greatest Fear

My greatest fear is that I write something
so clear that no one says anything at all

I simply drift away
like a leaf in the fall
and wait for the snow
to absorb the sound of the call
I never got
beneath the white of crystalline thought
I rot
irate in all I wrote

Suffering

Suffer
ring thy neck
lace those drugs
and dye
the hare that races our despair
will shelter the ones who care
asthmatic heir to the thrown stones
skip through scriptures
and kick the bones
how narrow the marrow of morrow
we burrow the sorrow we borrow

TransPyre

Serendipitous edge of shade I cast
does well to compel where my thoughts should dwell
serrated life lingers in jaded past
contortionist conscience is conscious hell

memory's prism refracts my true hue
how exquisite the guilt of axis tilt
to access myself I must think of you
and what transpired in the city we built

the roads were paved with ill intent to drive
away the things that cared so much for me
my burning hate for self is still alive
within the other half that you can't see

sometimes I feel this burn when I reflect
I cannot always be what you expect

BedLamb

We lie in the garden
then beg for a pardon
[but this lamb has no chops]
for Abraham only stops
if god directs

our god topples towers that man Erects
there shall be no head!
lest it be served on a silver platter

Baptist Lives Matter

A

Alas, strawman's pass laws and add a tax
small ants stab at fat rats as claws cat call
shabby shaman shams abash as a mask
and at last arms fall, as Atlas plays ball

The Phallus See

Nothing compares to the despair in flesh
arrogant gnats consume desires rot
pragmatic pigs purse their lips and refresh
as enamored sloth gets off and has not

callous hands ring the neck of fallacy
if nobody's home the dome shall crumble
one eyed monsters blind men, while phallus see
peg legs are the reason why we stumble

breasting waves of sirens sight just to lie
in beds of flowers planted just to pluck
a fate amassed by what we choose to tie
to what we earned and what just came as luck

suitors clamor just to hammer her clam
I fool them all, they know not who I am

Swans Spawn all Dawns

Hallmark apathy claws a sap apart
as cash pays a scam that spans tacky art
cards mask man's task [a lady always fawns]
and charms can't fall flat, as "swans spawn all dawns"

See Mental Health

How dense we are to dull the sense
cement all health to fit a mold
cracks propagate as we grow old
and concrete thoughts will crumble hence

This marble head doth shine sincere
and does not wax for polished feel
my imperfections make me real
I don't conceal what others fear

While others search for mantle peace
and pay the price for Matisse bust
I cast my stone at all they trust
and pray that mantis mantras cease

Silent Movie

As rows of seat are set up for a show no one can bear
a line is formed to shake the hands of friends who say they care
a child's regret and string quartet will weep a song of fate
as hearts dilate in final hour, flowers dilapidate

how oddly dense this audience that only sees the plot
this silent movie plays out as my flesh begins to rot

the energy that once was me can never be destroyed
the spirit of eternal soul will soon be redeployed
I do not know exactly where you might see me again
the question is far less an if and really more a when

A Case Can Be Made

We dial in on static in somatic search for grace
as voids converge on earthly urge to gnaw away our place
if nothing comes from nothing then what drives our will to dance
if all along the song was gone then how did we advance?

perhaps collapse of tower was a blessing for us all
we speak as one in serpent tongue and question why we fall

though poets think they're clever on things others overlook
they often tend to blather as they babble on a brook
the river does not care for words. its mouth serves other needs
and fires can be fed with books, yet everyone still reads

Wormwood

I sought to capture rapture through the aperture of youth
lo and behold I am quite old, and I still know not the truth
I swam inside the fountain, but I drowned to steal a cent
all mountains form to crumble but they never give consent

I spoke with god by payphone about nothing that I knew
I echoed ecce homophone, yet nothing said is new

this lamb was met with silent threat and heard the dial tone
I realized I myself was god and felt so all alone
I spoke like Zarathustra had to be misunderstood
if people will not feast on me, I wonder if wormwood

Fire Starter

The kindling in our craft of words is what we left unsaid
we feed the flame for famished fame and live a life unread
us pyrotechnic poets are the artists left unfed
pensive panic and manic laughter dance as kindred dread

our ashen passion smolders in the pyre of prose we pen
through smoke signals we call for help… then never seen again

provocative, yet paper thin, this whim behind the veil
as sonneteers we're arsonists, that blaze across the trail
phonetic is our etiquette that's fricative yet frail
the freest words that one can write are written from a jail

.

Sloth

"it is no surprise if his servants also disguise themselves as servants of righteousness"-**Somewhere in the bible**

It cannot be overstated, this thought
is nurturing weed worth letting tree rot?
No! The fruits of my labor are my own.
Surprise me not! you usurpers of throne

If beggar has power to rob men blind,
his hearts true intent was only to find
servants. These are the men that I despise.
Also, I loathe those that perpetuate lies

Disguise the harsh truth, they only care for
themselves. Give a man fish, he'll ask for more.
As for the ones that seek to say I'm cold
servants don't think, they just do as they're told

Of all the ways that Satan may appear,
righteousness is the form that all should fear.

Tear out the Page

To ravish the ravine between this dream
through words I so strung in unconscious stream
on walk you took with directionless feet
your head in a book with heart in retreat

you steady your hand to not lose you place
let language command this soul that you trace
lips salivate for loves intervention
whisper my words, you know my intention

read me out loud and brave to discover
the beauty that hides just beneath cover
boundless remains of poets reminding
be not afraid for words are not binding

say those three words that will make me concede
tear out our page and let no one else read

Serene

To learn of life, I sat beside this pond
I watched the reeds and thought of what to write
the fool who reads and thinks he has it right
is bound to never really have a bond

the great beyond that lurks beneath our nose
is rarely found in poetry or prose
reflect not on reflections you don't see
for written ripples can't disrupt what's free

for all the words one writes, what is "serene"?
no colors that we know can paint this scene
to see what I have seen and think to boast
explains why true beauty is lost on most

it's here I ponder stones I left unturned
and fondly though of bridges that I burned

Lions Made of Stone

Inspired by the words engraved upon the entrance to the rose garden at Lynch park

"Whosoever enters here, let him beware.
*   For he shall nevermore escape nor be free of my spell"*

I sit between the lions made of stone
and pet the weathered lines across their backs
they whisper in a tone I can't atone
for I alone have witnessed their attacks

On pedestals of bricks, they guard the land
well perched to prey on those who dare intrude
the garden grows and dies at their command
they curse all those who dance in interlude

for all the signs were there, yet we ignore
enchanted words were written on the wall
so callous is the call of lion's roar
the symphony of seasons seizes all

and I alone am privy to the throne
I sit between the lions made of stone

Sate in Would

I sat in woulds and sought out things to sate
how curious the things I contemplate
on plastic plate stochastic fate did drip
like clocks afraid to talk of fabrics rip

if undulating waves define the light
perhaps that means that there is finite right
but if that's true, man's future is confined
god chooses some and some are left behind

for seeds are sown but some will never take
mad hatters scatter nonsense just to make
poetic verse of flowers that we paint
but even god himself is not a saint

it's in the throes of volcanos we learn
that what we yearn is none of gods concern

Grain of Alt

We need the narratives to keep us safe
we cannot let the flock make judgement calls
opinions of dissent will only chafe
believe the truth society installs

as labyrinth lies about the labs emerge
you must believe we had the best intent
if politics and science don't converge
then we are justified in truth we bent

to keep you safe was always in our heart
that's why we made the thing that killed your mom
you're splitting hairs you shouldn't spilt apart
leave splitting things to those who made the bomb

To know that there are those who claim no fault
is why most view news with a grain of Alt

Hypocritical Grace Theory

Hypocritical grace queries the quagmire of the dire
as ethereal theories liberate our lucid flaw
communes hiss as poltergeist heist inspires need to conspire
pyres of pragmatic "truths" usher in a new age of law

sidelined by bodies lined in chalk, we kneel and talk of shock
collars of white and blue read how gavel refused to knock

and so, we knocked back, and burned it all down, for just one man
founders floundered, confounded by constant conflagration
and we continued to knock and burn to show that we can
unite as one for all those who fall within our nation

Truncate Temper

He how tends to the branch that extends
amends the shade that separates friends
and he who breaks or shakes for fruit
to dig up dirt beneath the root
should not be surprised when tree upends

Campy Ideology

Honest intent is not enough
when ideology becomes too campy

Unique Poetry

The froth of tards in fragments and shards
poets parrot tarot cards
and we laud over linguistic parlor trick
as they parlay word play with nothing to say
and waste away what little time we have in this world
on words
that are as empty as the nutsack
of a eunuch

Pro-Voice

While most will write profound insight to make the reader feel
I wish to write something so right that the reader thinks to steal
for if they with to steal it then I know it had a worth
my words impregnate fertile minds
you can't abort this birth

Pluminations

Will wind rescind its errant breeze
to ease the mind of feather caught
if zephyr heard the song of bird
than poetry would have no plot

unheard demands carry more weight
to change the fate of feathered fools
we build this nest of our unrest
a single plume can change the rules

l'enfer c'est les autres poétes

Kamikaze crafters: Pompous pilots that assault language
through arial alliteration (going over everyone's head)

the crucifixion of diction was slow
and our savior wore a crown of thorny prose

in the third stanza
he wrote again

perhaps the concept was sound
[phonctically speaking of course]
but once this religion of writing got organized
and saturated in the pagan traditions
of syllable count and rhyme scheme
it went right to hell

If Satan Sat in Place of God

greetings from down below, what doth hell owe
to a god that topples man's search for more?
heathens heave-ho and care not for the glow
for havens have not the luster of lore

clouded judgement reigns from the one above
flooding the world while he himself is dry
the great creator knows not how to love
and so I plan to set fire on high

so pull up a chair cause dis gon b good
chariots full of demons armed for war
carpenters will be burned with their own wood
as I goad god with my new threats of gore

it's clear that this god should be overthrown
so join me now so I may take the throne

Crafting Draft

A1 b A2 / a b A1 / a b A2 / A1 A2

As ever clever minds refine their craft
to polish stones that wiser men would skip
this poet tends to drift within a draft

while branching out from poetrees we graft
titanic thoughts will sink at iceberg tip
as ever clever minds refine their c*raft*

sin theRapists can't wait to give the shaft
we feud with Freud and wat to hear a slip
this poet tends to drift within a draft

as ever clever minds refine their craft
this poet tends to drift within a draft

Stark Angel

A1 b A2 / a b A1 / a b A2 / A1 A2 (inverse refrain couplet)

Darkness needs light, truth is in sight
balance is struck between both sides
starkness, our fear; words without might

a longing for blood leads to bite
the moon will howl as shadows hide
darkness needs light, truth is in sight

silent paws; claws foreshadow fight
silent pause, as flaws prey on pride
starkness, our fear, words without might

insight is truth, light needs darkness
might without words. fear our starkness

Fire Hoes

Form 27a

Indoctrinate through public teaching
truth segues to segregate
our politics is overreaching
program hate
indoctrinate

you're born from sin and here's our theory
if you're white you auto-win
all other races have grown weary
you're your skin
you're born from sin

if you oppose then you are evil
how do you not see the pros?
divisive words don't cause upheaval
fire hoes
if you oppose

Tangled in Heat

To tamper with thought of temperate day
and compare my love to the branches that sway
piss poor metaphors this poets pen pours
makes shiny armor of rusty amours

how timeless this love of starry eyed fate
devour the hourglass, don't hesitate
time is relative…I don't think *she* is
was this my test? have I failed the quiz

I write all of this from my shady seat
beneath the branches that tangled in heat

Cursa Major

Zeus overzealous in the fruit he doth bear
how tender and fair the plight of the jealous
desperate despair behind fear of affair
who tends to the bare grows wine from the trellis

Art be for the Horse

Splendors close
when we explain
splendid said
is dead end gain
windows cracked
so breeze is felt
I drew this shade
I hope you melt

Level Playing Field

I could speak at length
of glorified girth
but the dearth of your worth
brought death to our earth
let's unravel this gravel that gavel brough forth

we sought equal outcome
through mandate and law
yet yield of field revealed a flaw

science be damned
the maggots still gnaw
science be damned
the maggots still gnaw

Worth Knowing

How petty the pretty that destroys this city
the crack in cement from the flower is growing

and for those who make waves when no wind is blowing
if you must introduce yourself...
you aren't worth knowing

Hardy Plans

They visualize time as linear path
for they have yet to meet or feel its wrath
they have hardy plans in the seeds they sow
I work with the men who do not yet know

they speak of stages yet know not the play
they don't fear curtain will take them away
they swim in river yet don't see the flow
I work with the men who do not yet know

they see themselves as different than I
through chide they decided "his minds gone awry"
they speak of peak yet they stand on plateau
I work with the men who do not yet know

follow the fallow, with rest we may grow
I pause from my work...for I already know

Glossart

Ashes to ashes
dust to dust
…I combust.
swept up in this thought that consumes
all of those who dance with the brooms

I pen a glossary of bromides
to hide myself in
I gag myself
till paper thin
as I gin up ways to kill myself

gin up
gin down
gin up
…empty cup
solo
so low
so slow…this "process"

a loss of gloss as the glass shatters
and a love that was overrated
is serrated

I sit here elated
no one related

Loveless Time

the birds in me that sang in tree in effervescent joy
did cradle thoughts of future knots whilst whispering so coy
I understood life's meaning (it was written on her skin)
and so I stared so unprepared until I fell right in

ringing bells that rose in swells did bloom from my conviction
but age brough written rot out; dichotomy of diction

it scratches and attaches to the blind spots it will make
and it would take the breath of death or poetry of Blake

the birds in air cannot compare to fruit we bear with snake
although once sure that it was pure, that was my first mistake

Picking Scabs

We do not choose what cuts us
we can only pick our scabs

Save Venom of Snake

Save venom of snake, for nothing is pure
except all the pain true art must endure.
accept all the pain, true art must endure
poets wax/wane till the waves hit the sure

shed away comfort in the craft you make
for nothing is pure save venom of snake

O'Pine

Will the sap of sapiosexuals stick
or do the needles need less
opined the old prick

is the oak "a-okay" in all that I say
or do I lumber though thoughts
that got carried away

Macabrevity

To graze with god the stoics stow the wick of wicked ways
yet poets wax on melting clocks to colorize the grays

please grade me not for work I've done, for I am one with all
I had my fling with spring and then I fell into the fall
never compete, just take the L, and you will be complete
in macabre macarena, we dance with naked feet

Aphormai

We must admonish our brothers against all they admire
for man and nature are but one and share in divine fire
the wisest men know happiness is never found in things
the bird is only given worms and yet the bird still sings

in each of us, a halfway poem, that lives inside constraint
though canvas has a finite size, we choose just what to paint

but there are those that question art and lose their frame of mind
no colors can be virtuous if half the world is blind
place urinals on pedestals and tell me what it means
there is no point in anything…we live inside black screens

Convertigo

I try to convert the hurt
but all I do is kick up the dirt
and the muddy waters slaughter the laughter I'm after
before I can
skirt; the issue
before I can convert
I go

my hereditary *h*identity
this masculine amenity
a severed head
to get in the john
the my you won't see
is gone

This Suits Me

Even from the box where im stored
I can tell the kids are getting bored
it's been a long day
10 thousand dollars worth of lumber
as I succumb to the umber slumber
you stare at the number above
and where there used to be love
there is nothing
except a finite amount of tears
that will expire…like I have done

I know you will not forget
but the colder I am
the number you get

Grasping at Flaws

Detach from match and hatch a better plan
for audience knows not the flame they fan
while phantom fears still masquerade as want
I harbor unsure thoughts on peers to haunt

Very few will suffocate in sorrow
for audience knows not the flame they fan
burrowing the trinkets that they borrow
marrow sucked from bone, unknown tomorrow

Imaginary

Purposeless rat is prone to addiction
thoughts pay no rent and face no eviction
suffering is the cost of the living
sin comes in waves cos god likes forgiving

how graphic the gore as god plotted plan
tangential to the true terror of man
a slippery slop of hope that was spun
for god came as man to rise and then run

derivative deity "save me please!"
an integral prayer we say from our knees
help me be square with my roots of despair
how many apples does eve have to share?

while solving for X we never asked why
the number of the beast; lowercase i

Squoze

I pine for needles to sew thy seed
so cloth of moth may intercede
the May dismay of flowers grim
has pilfered day and brought the dim
mention this in metered line
but shun the shine upon the shrine
shhh…the rind is close behind
a slice of lemons life confined
aided by our search for the truth
devour sour days of youth
squeeze me now and ring me dry
propose to me so I may die

French Horns

Here I sit and wonder whether French horns torn
for the man its asked to mourn

morning tend to linger with a somber feel
disbelief that night is real

reeling from this movie, I act out in fear
casting calls no one can hear

Mite

leaves do not rest when they fall
they rustle in death
as stems build nests that spawn future songs
I pen my wrongs
and wrestle with the empty vessel of my untrue virtue
that chews through my might
bite after bite

Charlatans Webb

dissuade thy shade that shadow made
darkness comes in many a shape
and though you say you're unafraid
I see the hair that stands on nape

you found it when you sought escape
and now it seems that it has stayed
a ghastly sight with mouth agape
this carnival of fright conveyed

so fraught with though being caught
you never fly for fear of web
learned dread is fed and taught
forsake the flows that know no ebb

Bromides Keeper

if I capitulate to the poetry's populist movement
then virgin bride should open wide and let my bother slide in
let us share in this nightmare of societal impairment

circle jerk
around all social justice jizz
"what's mine is his!"
let's snowball this mess until you confess
that perhaps we went too far

or should we ask him to fuck her deeper?
as we hide behind a bromide
she chided "who's the keeper?"

Tomorrows Special

motherless flowers
sitting in yesterday's water
dilapidate from the wait of the previous day

their wilted will spills on the floor
making a colorful display
of their despair

they wait for a sign
to quell the tension

* NOW AT BARGAIN PRICES! *

Think on Me

I thought of how the leaves that fell lived on
and how the dew would kiss my feet at dawn
then wondered if the bugs that crawled on knee
had ever spent the time to think on me

Hear Hear

here here tiered tears
the meter of theater appears
[applaud]
and nod for your god

cheer my children
so everyone may know thy name
fan the flame and starve
for famine fame is thinly veiled
yet it has prevailed
and nothing can deter the carpenter when he starts to carve

Grape Culture

de-vine this comedy so misaligned
for grape culture leaves stains upon the sole
beneath the shade they prune the prudent mind

we press our lips right up to the bunghole
unabashed we drown ourselves in pleasure
for even empty barrels have a role

aerate areola at your leisure
for full bodied is the taste of our glass
burgundy the lips that have no measure

scantily clad and gladly decanting
as Trojan horse armies enter en masse
we whisper words that sound so enchanting

"That was good for me, how was it for you?
I love a dry wine, how bout a round two?"

The Brevity of Beau Idéal

The only thing more fleeting than beauty
is our love for beautiful things

One in the Chamber

Let us rue the things that will never set
like silver lining on a pirouette
a cold metal click
blood rushing
exhale
perhaps my next try won't end with a fail

Don't Quote Me

Art is the true hue of man without place
is there anything more tender to trace?
to wander in faceless and graceless gift
console the shadows in the shapes that shift

those who have hope, have not the faintest clue
who are they to know or judge what I do
are they trapped by frame or boundless in dance?
broken the mirror that reflects on the glance

by the time the paint dries the truth is gone
life reflects art for the ones who belong

Improve the Tale

We dial in on crock we made
to sever glad in everglade
how foolish the fish to swim on a whim
how quick this grin can turn to grim

The Price of Admission

A pause for applause will cause cadence to teeter
we fill up the seat to suckle on teat
if merit of meter is theater
our deceit and admission upon the receipt

although I find this worldly stage worth deserting
I'm afraid of hurting all those I know
I'm certain that I could curtail curtain
take spotlight off me…and carry on with the show

Say Lore

Shouting tongues twist
to the terror of wrist
author
write us
or rate us
keep this in tryst
bedlam bind us and blind us
eye in cyst
you cannot spell fascist without fist
the fog of boiling frog is fickle
like the hammer and sickle
…and the murder we missed

read sky in mourning
say lore
take warning

Hold Thresh

The thoughts we can't hold we thresh to break mold
our paper-thin sin gets lost in the fold
crumpled up poets that long to be heard
scribbling nonsense and sounding absurd
depart from deep art let heart start afresh
watch how the cuts are returning to flesh

Crumble

I keep searching through the ruin
of the life I keep on screwing
cause we're never quite so humble
as when the kingdom starts to crumble

I don't know what I'm doing
or what I'm saying
so I mumble
I've never tripped up on a lie
but with the truth I start to stumble

As the Wax Falls

At the candlelit vigil
in my memory
please return the concern
you didn't burn for me

and know, that as the wax falls
in the autumn air
I couldn't reach out in life
and that's why I'm not there

I flew as close as I could to the sun
but I only found darkness

Modicum in Me

Where do I begin my manic kin…?
There is nothing more unnerving than the verve behind ventriloquist
virtue. Dialogue that seeks to demonize others in an attempt to deify
the speaker is undeserving of decorum.

Surely, we can agree that surly speech is not tantamount to the
sermon on the mount. We must listen if we truly seek to surmount
ideological differences. A prudent teacher does not preach to the
student they seek to reach. a round of applause does not mean your
thoughts are without flaws.

Flies feast on feces
yet the gnat knows not what it gnaws

Cloudy Days

I'm quite ashamed of the time I have spent
in penning out words to sound eloquent
but since we first met, I've not been the same
I wish to say more than just "je vous aime"

how cursed this tongue that seeks for a verse
two lips can't speak whilst they quiver and purse
I wish to drop guard and let garden bloom
yet cowardice lets unspoken love loom

consuming this thought of all I have not
I'd spout it all out, yet doubt hath me caught
entangled in weeds I languish in speech
should I borrow words like linguistic leech?

how do I love thee? Let me count the ways
thou art temperate on my cloudy days

Dew

I saw the grass that grew in shade
and asked her why she carried blade
She spoke to me
"What do you mean....
are you new to life...? you seem quite green"

I saw the ant that built the hill
and asked if work had brought him thrill
He looked at me
but couldn't say
then bowed his head and marched away

I wept out loud from what I saw
I knew my nature, yet knew not law
"what should I do?"
I asked the dew

      "dew onto others... as I dew to you"

Gold Leaves (Gilt)

I see the boughs bow beneath weight of snow
and think to myself "what does this tree know?"
how foolish the flower...choosing to wilt
as beauty leaves, all that glitters is gilt

the folly of age is printed on page
umber the slumber; we lumber on stage
nothing gold can stay, say silver of tongue
serrated by the serenades unsung

unhappy with image...colors alter
why is it always in fall we falter?
severing roots, we try to be limber
yet truncate our stay as we sway.... timber

guiltless the beauty that selfishly jumped
leaving family trees in the cool breeze... stumped

Alone… Alone…

I fear the morrow will not be merry
yet steer my sorrow as if to bury
bone bereft of marrow

To what do I owe that which I don't know
will shall wilt within the straight and narrow

These stones that lay unturned still yearn for flight
they fragment sense of self to sharpen bite
directionless arrow

To what do I owe that which I don't know
will shall wilt within the straight and narrow

No head of stone can atone for the moan I own
the silence screams
alone...alone...

Rhapsody I

Am I to lie of this *rhapsody, I*
fly by night for my nature is absurd
hide away the *mania* and deny

I know that I am happy in the sky
reflections of myself show I'm a bird
am I to lie of this rhapsody eye?

I cannot sing or seek of sirens sigh
and that is why I lean on slanted word
Hide away the *mania* and deny

these painted feathers never seem to dry
the not so early bird will go unheard
am I to lie of this rhapsody eye?

to wrestle with these thoughts and wonder why
I nestle between lines that feel so blurred
hide away the *mania* and deny

I wish to forsake flock yet can't decry
cowed by herd I fear I am a cowherd
am I to lie of this *rhapsody, I*
hide away the *mania* and deny

Footnote:

...because you (the reader)
are too fucking dumb to figure out anything
unless it's explained to the point where beauty is lost...

"Rhapsody I" is an anagram for dysphoria and *"mania"* is an anagram for "anima"

Cicada's Serenade

Let mantis mantra fade in the mosquito masquerade
a charlatan's charade doth hide in cloth the moth has frayed
by breaking ebb and flow in all the truths I cannot show
my locust lust has stayed in the cicada's serenade

how merry is the mite that seeks to write of loves first bite?
a million ayes to cite and yet you wouldn't share in flight

if fluid thoughts should thaw into reflections that I saw
then love me gnats would gnaw upon this decomposing flaw
my locust lust has stayed in the cicada's serenade
yet fleshy truths seem raw…I cannot shed so I withdraw

Made in the USA
Columbia, SC
09 December 2021

50848623R00078